10-Minute Energy-Saving Secrets

10-Minute Energy-Saving Secrets

250 Easy Ways to Save Big Bucks Year Round

Jerri Farris

FAIR WINDS
PRESS
GLOUCESTER, MASSACHUSETTS

Text © 2005 by Fair Winds Press

First published in the USA in 2006 by
Fair Winds Press, a member of
Quayside Publishing Group
33 Commercial Street
Gloucester, MA 01930

10 09 08 07 06   1 2 3 4 5

ISBN 1-59233-245-5

Library of Congress Cataloging-in-Publication Data available

Cover Design by Laura Shaw Design
Cover Illustration by Elizabeth Cornaro
Book design by Leslie Haimes
Printed and bound in USA

To my children, Evan and Katie, who are the lights of my life.

Table of Contents

Knowledge is Power

The latest headlines are filled with news of devastating hurricanes, the looming oil crisis, and global warming. Meanwhile, in our hometowns, natural gas prices are skyrocketing and the price of gasoline ricochets daily. Even for people who aren't political or environmental activists, it's understood that the world's energy issues are no longer abstract matters, they're concrete problems that affect our wallets and our daily lives. It's easy to feel helpless in the face of all this, but we're not. Every one of us has the power to both reduce our energy bills and have a positive impact on the planet.

How can we claim this power? We can learn the energy-saving secrets in this book, put them to use in our own lives, and share them with others. Today, each one of us can unplug a countertop appliance we're not using, switch off a light as we leave the room, or fill our tires with air. This weekend, we can pick up a can of expandable foam, a tube of caulk, or a compact fluorescent bulb, and reduce the cost of heating, cooling, or lighting our homes. Over time, we can purchase energy-efficient appliances and automobiles, weatherstrip and insulate our windows and doors, and develop life long energy-saving habits.

Secret Benefits of Energy Saving

Purchasing new, energy-efficient windows, doors, or appliances has an immediate impact on your utility bills, just as buying a fuel-efficient car immediately reduces the money you spend on gasoline. What most people don't know is this: Some utility companies offer rebates on the purchase of Energy Star appliances, certain states allow tax deductions on those same purchases, and the federal government offers tax deductions on energy-saving home improvements and purchases. To take advantage of these added benefits, check with your utility company before buying a major appliance, consult an accountant about the tax advantages of making your home more energy efficient, and save all related receipts. You may be surprised at all the ways the ideas in this book pay off for you.

The Time is Now

The secrets are now in your hands—the rest is up to you. Pick a chapter and put at least one of the ideas into action today. When you see how easy it is, you'll be ready to dive right into a new, more energy-efficient, way of life.

PART ONE

Indoor Essentials

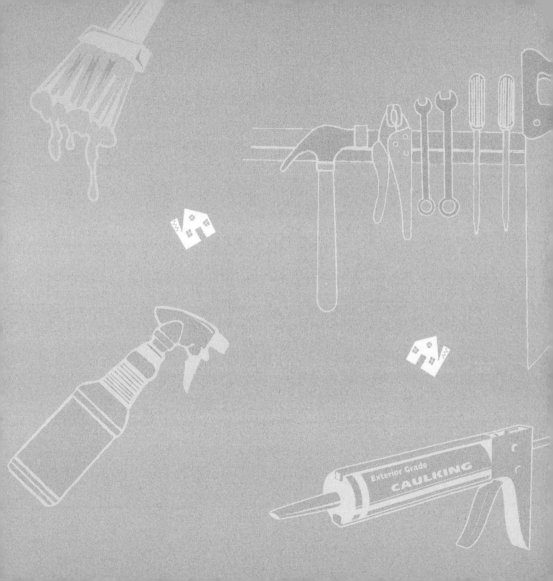

Chapter 1

Windows and Doors

According to the Energy Information Administration, a unit of the Department of Energy, about one third of the heat loss in a typical home occurs through windows and doors. To help keep heat inside your home, use the tips that follow to weatherproof and insulate your windows and doors. It doesn't take much time and it quickly pays for itself!

Seal gaps around windows.

Gaps around windows let conditioned air out and outside air in, which costs you money. To seal the window casings, the wood trim around windows, apply a bead of silicone caulk to the joint between the casing and the wall. Using the right caulk helps it blend in—clear caulk is typically best for stained trim or dark colors of paint; white or almond blends well with most shades of white.

Weatherstrip casement windows.

High-quality casement windows are energy efficient, but you can improve their efficiency even more by installing self-adhesive foam or rubber compression strips on the outside edges of the window stops.

Weatherstrip the sides of double-hung windows.

First, scrape excess paint from the sashes and the windowsill. Cut vinyl V-channel to fit in the channel on each side of the window frame, long enough to reach two inches past the closed position for each sash. (Be sure the V-channel won't cover the sash closing mechanisms.)

Weatherstrip the tops and bottoms of double-hung windows.

Clean the lower edge of the bottom sash. When the sash is completely dry, attach self-adhesive compressible foam. Next, lift the bottom sash and pull down the top sash.

Position metal V-channel on the bottom rail of the top sash, with the open end of the V pointed downward. Nail the V-channel in place, and then flare it out to fill the gap between the sashes.

Seal window sashes.

During extremely cold or hot weather when you wouldn't open your windows anyway, temporarily sealing them closed is a small sacrifice you can make to generate big savings. A window sash—the frame that surrounds the glass—can leak air. To seal the gap around the sash, close and lock the window, then put clear, peelable caulk strips between the sash and the window frame. When the weather improves and you want to open the windows, peel off the caulk and you're all set.

Lock the windows.

Even if you're not concerned about security, keep your windows locked during heating and cooling season. Locking a casement window pulls the sash tight against the frame and helps reduce drafts. Locking a double-hung window pulls the sashes closer together and blocks airflow.

Select the best window treatment for the job.

Choose your window treatments wisely and you'll save big on heating and cooling costs. High-quality honeycomb shades with a triple cell construction, for example, are very efficient insulators, especially on windows with only one treatment. These shades can increase the energy efficiency of a single-paned window by five times, and a double-paned window by more than two times.

QUICK TIP

White-colored shades are best for regions with warm summers because they help reflect heat away from your home.

Dress your windows in layers.

In cold weather, most of us instinctively dress in layers because it helps us keep warm. Not surprisingly, dressing a window in layers helps a room stay warm, too, and for exactly the same reason. Air retains heat, so each layer of a window treatment traps some heated air in the room. In the summer, layered window treatments provide buffers between hot outdoor air and cool indoor air. Blinds or shades covered by sheers and topped by drapes are not only stylish, but also energy efficient.

QUICK TIP

When selecting draperies, buy lined versions whenever possible. Linings help insulate the window and protect the drapery fabric from sun damage.

Super size your curtains and drapes.

Buy drapes, blinds, and shades that are big enough to cover the frame as well as the window itself. That way, they cut air infiltration around the trim as well as through the glass. For optimum insulation, let drapes rest below the windowsill or—even better—hang all the way to the floor.

QUICK TIP

Valences and cornice boards add another layer of insulation above a window. Use them wherever possible.

Replace inefficient or damaged windows.

If your home still has single-paned windows, it's time for them to go. It may seem like you can't afford to replace them, but actually, you can't afford not to replace them. New triple-pane windows lose 75 percent less heat than single-panes. That means lower energy bills for years to come. Be sure to replace any damaged windows as well: If condensation collects inside a double-paned window or if the glazing no longer holds the glass securely in the sash, it's time for something new.

QUICK TIP

When shopping for energy-efficient windows, look for the Energy Star logo and a National Fenestration Council rating. By evaluating this information, you can more easily compare the energy efficiency of the units you're considering.

Weatherstrip around storm windows.

If you have storm windows, you can radically improve their efficiency with a little weatherstripping. Before hanging the storm windows, attach foam compressions strips to the storm window stops on the exterior window frame. When the storm windows are in place, fill any gaps between the window and the exterior trim with caulk backer rope, weatherstripping foam designed to fill wide cracks.

Eliminate moisture trapped between storm and permanent windows.

Water is an efficient conductor of heat, so when moisture is trapped between the windows, energy is being wasted. To let the moisture escape, drill one or two small holes through the bottom rail of the storm window.

Install window insulation kits.

These inexpensive kits include plastic sheeting or shrink-wrap plastic to cover the inside of your window. Many kits recommend that you warm the plastic with a hair dryer to tighten it and remove any wrinkles. Read and follow the manufacturer's directions to install.

Caulk around basement window frames.

Small basement windows are easy to overlook, but it's just as important to keep them airtight as it is any other window. From the outside, use exterior caulk or expandable foam to fill the gaps between the window and the surrounding block or concrete.

Take advantage of the sun in the winter.

On sunny days, open the blinds and drapes on the south and west sides of the house. The sun will help warm the rooms at absolutely no cost, as long as you remember to close the drapes and blinds when the sun sets.

Block out the sun on hot days.

Close the blinds and drapes, especially on the south and west sides of the house, on sunny, summer days. Deflecting the sun prevents solar gain.

Fill cracks in wood entrance doors.

Cracks in wood doors leak an unbelievable amount of air!
Luckily, they're easy to fix. Work from inside the room. On
painted doors, fill the cracks with wood filler or caulk. On
stained doors, use tinted wood putty. Then sand the area and
touch up the paint or stain.

Paint or seal your wood doors.

Unless all the edges of a wood door are finished, it expands
and contracts with the weather, which encourages cracks to
form. To prevent this from happening, paint or seal all the
edges of the door—including the top and bottom. You can find
high-quality wood sealers in the parts department of a hardware store or home center, or at any paint retailer.

Block drafts with a door sweep.

Without a door sweep to block it, cold air can easily swoop between the bottom of an entry door and the threshold. To replace or add a door sweep, start by measuring the door so you can buy one that fits. Next, tack or tape the sweep in place on the inside of the door, positioning it to touch the floor but not interfere with the door's ability to open and close. Drill pilot holes and drive screws to hold the sweep in place.

QUICK TIP

Avoid thresholds with built-in weatherstripping. On most, the weatherstripping wears out quickly, leaving gaps beneath the door.

Weatherstrip exterior doors.

Worn or missing weatherstripping costs you money every day.
Self-adhesive products are easy to use, but it's really worth the
effort to install metal weatherstripping. Measure the height and
width of the door and cut metal V-channel to fit. Tack the strips
to the doorjamb and the header, inside the stops. To keep the
channel from buckling, work from the top down. When the
strips are in place, use a putty knife to pull them into position,
between the door and the jambs, when the door is closed.

QUICK TIP

Be sure to add weatherstripping to the door between the
garage and the house to prevent cold or warm air from
infiltrating the house.

Weatherproof sliding glass doors.

Apply a self-adhesive foam compression weatherstripping to the edge of the doorjamb of a sliding glass door. Now you've taken care of the edges. Unfortunately, the broad expanse of glass that makes these doors so appealing also makes them inefficient when it comes to energy. Good window treatments, such as insulated shades or thermal film, can help.

Make sure exterior doors close tightly.

A door that doesn't shut tightly can allow inside air to escape. Adjust the door latch and strike plate on exterior doors to make sure they close as tightly as possible. Open and close the door, and watch the action between the bolt on the door and the strike plate, or catch, on the frame. If they're not aligned and working smoothly, try to determine which part is causing the problem. If the strike plate needs to be higher, drive 3-inch wood screws into the top of the doorjamb to pull up the doorframe; if it needs to be lower, drive the screws into the bottom of the jamb to pull the doorframe down. If the problem appears to be with the latch bolt, remove the door and set it aside. To raise the latch bolt, install thin cardboard shims behind the bottom hinge so it raises the whole door. To lower the door and the latch bolt, install shims under the top hinge.

QUICK TIP

Adding a storm door reduces drafts around the door and makes the area more comfortable, but storm doors and their installation are expensive, which makes the payback period comparatively long. Before investing in a storm door, investigate prices and consult your energy suppliers regarding the efficiency of a storm door in your climate.

Weatherstrip the bottom of a garage door.

Garage door weatherstripping, which comes in rolls, is usually displayed with other door hardware in hardware and home centers. To install it, open the garage door until the bottom is within comfortable reach. Pry off the old weatherstripping and remove the nails. Nail the new piece and in place. When you reach the edge of the door, cut the weatherstripping to fit.

QUICK TIP

If you're like me, you come in and out through the garage door, even when it's not necessary. The problem is, opening that big, heavy garage door uses up electricity and allows hot or cold air to infiltrate the garage, where it then tries to find ways inside the house. During heating and cooling seasons, avoid using the overhead garage door as an entrance or exit.

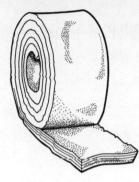

Chapter 2

Insulation

It's no secret that proper insulation is a critical factor in reducing energy costs, but it takes a savvy homeowner to recognize where insulation is most needed. These tips will help you evaluate the effectiveness of your current home insulation and target overlooked problem areas in your home.

Add insulation to floors above unheated spaces.

Floors above unheated spaces, like basements and crawlspaces, can be icy cold in the winter if they're not well insulated from below. If you have unusually cold floors in a room on the first floor, check below the floor for insulation. If you don't find any, have it added.

QUICK TIP

Installing insulation isn't a ten-minute job, but it's not difficult. Consider doing it yourself, using fiberglass batts. Make sure the batts fill the joist cavities completely, that they hug the floor above them, and that if the insulation has a paper or foil backing, the backing faces the heated, occupied part of the house. Secure the batts with string or wire supports.

Add insulation in your walls.

Consistently outrageous energy bills may be a sign that your house isn't adequately insulated, especially if it's an older home. To see if you need more wall insulation, find a flashlight and go to the main service panel. Shut off the power, and then take the flashlight to a light switch on an outside wall. Remove the cover plate and shine the flashlight into the space between the switch box and the wall. Take a look at the insulation there and estimate its thickness. If you don't find any insulation or what you do find seems inadequate, consult a professional insulation contractor. When you're finished, replace the cover plate and restore the power.

Add insulation to your attic.

First, check to see whether your attic is adequately insulated. Take a steel or wooden ruler into your attic and measure the depth of the insulation between the support beams, or joists. If you find six inches or less of insulation, consult an insulation contractor to see if you should add more. Utility companies in most climates recommend an insulation grade of at least R-50 for attic insulation (the 'R' stands for resistance to heat flow). Because insulation plays such a critical part in protecting the structure of your house and maintaining lower energy bills, it's usually best to hire a professional for this kind of project.

ENERGY SAVER ALERT

Shop around for an insulation contractor. Get recommendations from friends, relatives, neighbors, insulation suppliers,
and home centers. Get bids and check references from at
least three contractors. Before making a final decision, pick
up a Federal Trade Commission fact sheet from a local home
center or insulation supplier. Ask the contractor to show you
his or her calculations for proper density, and then check
those calculations against the fact sheet.

Insulate the area above a rim joist.

The rim joist is the large board (usually a 2x10 or a 2x12) at the top of your foundation walls, the board to which the floor joists are connected. In many unfinished basements or crawl-spaces, the area between the rim joist and the floor sheathing isn't insulated. You can take care of this problem remarkably quickly. Buy several batts of fiberglass insulation at your local home center (ask for unfaced, R-19 insulation). Locate the rim joist in your basement or crawlspace. Cut the insulation into strips and push the strips into the cavities above the rim joist. NOTE: Be sure to wear long sleeves, heavy pants, gloves, safety glasses, a hat, and a dust mask or respirator when working with fiberglass insulation.

Seal cracks and holes in interior walls.

There is always at least a small crack where two building mate-rials meet. Make it your goal to fill these cracks to keep conditioned air from flowing in and out. These are some key areas where you may find cracks or openings: around kitchen and bathroom cabinets, around fireplaces, under counter ledges, and along the edges of your countertops. If you find any unfilled openings during your search, fill them with high-quality caulk.

Seal mechanical openings.

The openings for water spigots, gas lines, electric service, phone and data lines leak air unless they're filled in some way. It's easy, inexpensive, and very cost-effective to plug them with expandable foam. If an opening already has filler but it's cracked or crumbling, use a utility knife to cut it out. When you've completely gotten rid of the old filler, spray expandable foam into the opening.

QUICK TIP

Whenever practical or possible, spray the expanding foam from inside rather than outside the house—it creates a tighter seal.

Fill kitchen and bathroom drainpipes.

Check under your bathroom or kitchen sink. Odds are, the hole for the drainpipe is a lot larger than the pipe itself, and the area around the pipe is leaking air like crazy. If the hole is really big, you may have to stuff it with caulk backer rope before you add the expandable foam. If it's more moderately sized (as most are), simply spray the foam into the opening and let it dry.

Chapter 3

Appliances

Appliances account for about 20 percent of the energy used by a typical household. Buying and using them wisely can make a significant impact on your energy bills.

Refrigerators

Set your refrigerator to the right temperature.

Keep your refrigerator's thermostat set between 37 and 40°F and the freezer set between 0 and 5°F. Setting the thermostat just 10°F below these levels costs a mint. In fact, those 10°F can increase a refrigerator's energy usage by as much as 25 percent.

Clean your refrigerator coils.

Refrigerator coils are magnets for dust and dirt. Just because no one can see the dust and dirt doesn't mean you don't need to clean them. Dirty coils force the refrigerator motor to work harder, which keeps your fridge from running efficiently. To clean the coils, pull the refrigerator away from the wall and unplug it. (The refrigerator should roll easily. If it doesn't, look for the problem rather than dragging the unit.) Use a brush attachment on a vacuum cleaner to clean dust and lint from the coils on the back of the unit. Next, remove the plastic panel on the front of the refrigerator, at the bottom. Typically, this panel snaps off, but you may need to remove a couple screws to get it off. Use a crevice attachment to clean the coils behind the panel. Clean the floor, plug the refrigerator in, and roll it back into position.

Get a grip on your gasket.

The doors on refrigerator and freezer doors have rubber gaskets that seal the cold air inside. If a gasket is worn out, the compressor has to work overtime to keep up, which is expensive and puts more demand on the unit. Check seals for cracks or damage a couple of times a year. To test a seal, close the refrigerator or freezer door on a sheet of paper. When you pull the paper out, you should feel the gasket gripping it. If it slips out without resistance, the gasket may need to be replaced. Consult a repairperson to do the actual replacement.

QUICK TIP

If the door gasket is damaged or completely shot, consider replacing the unit. Some experts say that new gaskets rarely work effectively, and new refrigerators are much more energy efficient than older models. Replacing a 10-year-old refrigerator can reduce your electric bills up to $40 a year.

Level with your refrigerator.

A refrigerator compressor pumps refrigerant through the coils. This action requires more energy when the refrigerator is not level. Refrigerators are designed to tilt backwards just a little so the doors naturally swing closed. However, they still need to be level from side to side. To check, set a level across the top of your refrigerator unit, near the front and running from right to left. If the bubble on the level is in the center of the black lines, the refrigerator is level. If not, you need to adjust the front feet. Pull off the lower panel on the front of the refrigerator and find the feet. If the bubble is off to the right, you'll want to raise the right foot or lower the left. If it slopes to the left, you'll need to do the opposite. To adjust the feet, use an adjustable wrench to turn the screw. Turn the screw clockwise to lower a foot, counterclockwise to raise it. Make adjustments until the bubble is directly in the center of the window.

Calculate and compare.

If you have your heart set on a new appliance and have reasons
for making the investment beyond the energy efficiency of a
new model, by all means take the leap. However, if your main
reason for considering the investment is energy efficiency, you
should know exactly how much your current model costs to
run. Check your most current electricity bill to find cost of a
kilowatt-hour of electricity. Next, check your appliance's serial
plate and look for the wattage. (If the wattage isn't listed, check

for amps and volts. Multiplying the amps by the volts gives you the wattage.) Multiply the appliance's wattage by the hours it will be in operation each month. Divide this number by 1,000. The number you get is the number of kilowatt-hours the appliance uses each month. Finally, multiply the kilowatt-hours by the rate your electric company charges. The result is the cost of running the appliance for a month. Compare this to the cost of running a new model and consider how long it will take for the energy savings to equal your investment in a new model.

CALCULATE THE MONTHLY COST OF USING AN APPLIANCE

Step 1: [WATTAGE (amps x volts)] x [# hours appliance is in use every month] : 1,000 = kWh (kilowatt hours) per month

Step 2: [Cost of a kWh of electricity (based on your most current electric bill)] x kWh per month = monthly cost of running appliance

Know the facts before you buy: Side-by-side refrigerator/
freezer models use about 7 to 13 percent more electricity
than freezer-on-top or freezer-on-bottom models. Although
through-the-door dispensers and automatic icemakers seem
like a good idea from an energy standpoint, many utility
companies warn that they actually increase energy usage.

Unplug unused refrigerators.

Unplugging an old, unused refrigerator takes just a second,
but it can save up to $170 a year! Just remember to store
your unused refrigerator safely, so children can't get trapped
inside. Padlock the door closed or block the door open to
keep kids safe.

Turn off the anti-sweat switch.

During hot, humid weather, condensation can form on the exterior of a refrigerator. Many newer models feature an anti-sweat mode that heats the area around the door seals to prevent that condensation. If your unit has an anti-sweat switch, turn it off in the winter and leave it off, even in the summer, unless you see moisture around the door seals. If it becomes necessary to turn the switch back on, use it only as long as necessary.

Reposition your refrigerator.

Refrigerators should be positioned away from heat sources, such as ovens, heat registers, and windows that receive direct sunlight. Allow at least two inches of clearance around the unit so air can circulate around the condenser coils and disperse the heat they generate.

Shut the refrigerator door.

Cool air spills out every time you open the refrigerator door.
Before cooking, decide what you're going to need from the
refrigerator. Open the door once to remove the ingredients and
once to replace them.

Keep your freezer full.

Whether you see it as half full or half empty, it's more expensive to maintain a partially filled freezer than a full one. If your freezer isn't filled with food, freeze water in milk cartons or plastic bottles to help it stay cold.

Defrost the freezer regularly.

Ice crystals in a freezer reduce its efficiency. You should always defrost a freezer before it builds up a quarter inch of frost.

Ovens and Cooktops

Don't overuse your oven self-cleaning cycle.

Depending on how well insulated your oven is and how much you pay for energy, it can cost as much as $1 to run the self-cleaning cycle. Cutting back is easy: get an inexpensive silicone oven liner. You can wipe off minor spills in one swipe. More serious spills may require an actual washing, but either way, you can keep the oven floor sparkling clean with very little effort.

Give the self-cleaning cycle a head start.

If or when you do use the self-cleaning cycle, start it right after baking something. The leftover heat will help jumpstart the cleaning process.

Thaw frozen food before cooking it.

Cool food cooks faster than frozen food. Several hours before you plan to cook a frozen casserole or other frozen dish, move it to the refrigerator to thaw. (Don't thaw food at room temperature—dangerous bacteria may develop.)

Put a lid on every pot.

Put lids on pots and pans when cooking on the stovetop, especially when bringing water to a boil. Lids increase cooking efficiency by 8 to 14 percent.

Cook under pressure.

Pressure cookers reduce cooking times as much as 50 to 75 percent. Unlike your grandmother's touchy little number, today's pressure cookers are safe, efficient, and easy to use.

Plan energy-efficient meals.

Cook everything for a meal in the oven or in one pot whenever possible. Some of my family's favorite meals are collections of baked dishes, such as meatloaf, baked potatoes, and green bean casserole, or pot roast with potatoes and carrots.

Don't overfill the oven.

Keep the heat inside your oven circulating efficiently by leaving two inches between pans and between pans and the sides and front of the oven. The more efficiently the heat circulates, the faster the food cooks.

When you make a casserole or other oven dish, make enough for two meals: one for that day and another for the freezer. That way, all you have to do the second time around is slide the casserole in the microwave for a few minutes, and voila, dinner's ready.

Use your toaster oven.

By virtue of being smaller than regular ovens, toaster ovens are much more economical to operate. Whenever possible, use a toaster oven—they use one-third to one-half as much energy as full-sized ovens.

Use your oven's convection mode.

A convection oven has a fan inside that helps to circulate heat quickly and evenly throughout the oven. Today's ovens sometimes feature a convection mode. This mode enables you to cook foods in 10 percent less time at temperatures 25 percent lower than the conventional baking mode. The Department of Energy estimates that convection ovens are 23 percent more efficient than conventional ovens.

Shine your burner bowls.

If you have electric burners with reflector bowls, keep those bowls clean. Dirty bowls absorb heat, while shiny, reflective bowls direct more of the burner's heat to the pots and pans. Consider buying new bowls, if necessary. Buy the best ones you can find at a local home center, hardware store, or the housewares department of a discount store.

Leave the oven door closed during cooking.

Have you ever noticed that the element clicks on every time you check on whatever's cooking? That's because 20 percent of the oven's heat escapes when you open the door. Develop the habit of using the timer and turning on the oven light rather than opening the door while baking.

Give your oven a break and fire up the grill.

Grilling is one of the reasons why living is easy in the summer time. It's simple and it makes food delicious. Best of all, your air conditioner doesn't have to strain to keep up with the heat created by the oven or stovetop.

Share the warmth when you cook.

When temperatures fall in the autumn, my family starts anticipating the soups and stews and roasts and desserts that traditionally follow. A pot of soup simmering on the stove fills the house with fragrance and warmth all afternoon. Baking can also contribute some warmth to the house: Leave the door ajar after you turn off the oven, and let that heat fill the room.

QUICK TIP

Although you might as well let a warm oven heat the room after cooking, don't turn on the oven just to warm up a cold room. It's terribly inefficient, and therefore, extremely expensive.

Select your burners wisely when cooking.

When cooking on the stovetop, select a burner that's about an inch smaller than the pot or pan you're using. That way, all of the energy will be absorbed by the cookware and the heat will be used most efficiently.

Replace warped pots and pans.

If you're using warped pots and pans on electric elements or a closed cooktop, you're wasting energy. A flat-bottom pan requires just two-thirds the amount of energy a warped pan requires.

Buy an induction stovetop.

If you're shopping for a new stovetop, consider an induction model. They heat up and cool down quickly and they cook very efficiently. You may also need to buy new, compatible cookware for the induction stovetop, so be sure to factor that into the equation.

Keep your gas burners firing.

Keeping the burners clean and the gas orifices open helps gas burners work efficiently. The flames should be blue—if they're yellow, something is amiss. Check for burned-on food stuck in the holes. If necessary, remove the burner and use a thin wire to clean out the holes. If the flames are still yellow after a thorough cleaning, have a repairperson adjust them.

Bake in glass and ceramic pans.

Glass and ceramic pans transfer heat very efficiently—you can turn down the oven temperature by 25°F and the food will cook in the same amount of time.

Limit oven preheat times.

Preheating longer than necessary is a waste of energy, but the baking process requires it. To save energy, turn on your oven just five to ten minutes before you're ready to put in the food.

Turn off the oven as soon as you're done.

Most of us have baked something and then come back an hour or two later only to realize that we left the oven on. You'll save money and enjoy more peace of mind if you can remember to turn off the oven right after you remove a finished dish.

Maintain oven seals.

Inside the oven door, there's a gasket that helps seal the heat inside. When that gasket gets frayed or worn, heat leaks out. Replace worn gaskets as soon as you notice them and before they become a bigger issue.

Heat and reheat foods in the microwave.

As a general rule, it's more efficient to use the microwave when heating beverages or small meals. The larger the meal, the less efficient a microwave becomes in comparison to using an oven to heat and reheat foods.

Clean your microwave oven.

Wipe out your microwave frequently—a clean microwave cooks faster than one filled with spills and splatters.

Dishwashers

Location, location, location.

Avoid installing the dishwasher next to the refrigerator, if possible. The heat and moisture from a dishwasher increases the energy consumption of a refrigerator. If they must be next to one another, separate them with a sheet of foam insulation.

Stop hand washing dishes.

Thanks-be-to-technology, running a dishwasher actually uses less energy than washing dishes by hand. According to a recent Ohio State University study, energy-efficient models use almost six fewer gallons of water per load than you would use washing the same number of dishes by hand. Using six fewer gallons of water means heating six fewer gallons of water, and that saves energy.

Replacing a 10-year-old dishwasher can save up to $44 a year on energy bills.

Rinse dishes in cold water.

Cold water works just as well as hot water for rinsing away most foods, and it's a lot cheaper.

Avoid using your dishwasher's "rinse-hold" feature.

The rinse-hold feature on a dishwasher uses three to seven gallons of hot water, which significantly raises the price for rinsing dishes.

Fill your dishwasher before running it.

A dishwashing cycle uses the same amount of hot water, no matter how many dishes are inside it. Waiting until the dishwasher is full reduces the number of times it's run, which reduces the energy used to run the dishwasher itself as well as the energy used to heat the water.

Let the dishes air dry.

Most dishwashers have a setting for air-drying. If yours does, use it. Unless you have a mold problem, simply leave the door ajar and let the dishes dry.

Washing Machines and Dryers

Use the max extract cycle on the clothes washer.

The more water in the clothes when you put them in the dryer, the longer it takes to dry them. The max extract mode on your washing machine lengthens the spin cycle and gets your clothes extra dry. Be sure to use this mode if you have it.

ENERGY SAVER ALERT

A regular load of laundry should dry in about forty minutes. If your dryer takes a long time to dry one load, your washing machine may not be running efficiently—the spin cycle may be leaving too much water in the load. To check, fill the washer and set the dial for the final spin. Let the cycle run for about ninety seconds, then check the tub: All the water should have drained out. If there's still water in the tub, have a repairperson adjust the spin cycle.

Wash clothes in cold water.

Unless the clothing is heavily stained, wash it in cold water using a detergent recommended for cold-water washing. This super-simple step can save the average family up to $70 a year. ninety percent of the cost of washing clothes comes from heating the water, so a hot-wash, warm-rinse cycle costs fifteen times as much as a cold-wash, cold-rinse cycle.

Presoak your dirtiest clothes.

Fifteen minutes of presoaking and five minutes of agitation get clothes cleaner than fifteen minutes of agitation.

Keep detergent to a minimum.

Carefully follow the manufacturer's directions regarding the amount of detergent you should use. Excessive detergent makes extra suds and those suds cause a washer to work harder and use more energy.

QUICK TIP

A new, horizontal-axis (front-loading) washer can save up to $90 a year compared to a five-year-old, top-loading washer. Front-loading washers use about half the energy and water of an equally sized top-loading washer.

Don't stuff your washer or dryer.

Fill up your washing machine, but don't overstuff it. When it comes to drying that oversized load, it will take much longer.

Do a few loads of laundry in a row.

Doing several loads of laundry, one after another, is cheaper than doing a load here and there. Drying consecutive loads takes advantage of built-up heat in the dryer, which saves energy.

Use your dryer's advanced shut-off features.

If your dryer has a humidity sensing shut-off or a temperature-sensing control, use them. Compared to the traditional timed shut-off, a humidity sensing shut-off uses 15 percent less energy and a temperature-sensing shut-off uses about 10 percent less energy.

Another great energy-saving laundry idea: Remove clothing when it's partially dry and let it air dry. You'll use less energy drying the clothes and you'll also avoid having to iron them!

Remove lint from your dryer filter.

Lint restricts the flow of air through the filter, and restricted airflow reduces efficiency. That explains why it costs 30 percent more to run a dryer with a dirty filter. Save yourself some money by cleaning the filter after every load.

Clean your electric dryer vents.

Dryer lint is extremely flammable so keep dryer vents clean not only to improve efficiency but also to prevent fires. At least once a year—once a season if you do lots of laundry—clean the dryer's vent system. Unplug the dryer or turn off the power to the circuit. Pull the dryer away from the wall and disconnect the vent hose from the wall vent as well as the dryer itself. Use the brush attachment on a vacuum cleaner to remove dust and lint from inside the dryer. (You may have to take off the back panel. Check the owner's manual for instructions.) Use the vacuum cleaner or a lamb's wool duster to clean out the vent hose. Replace the hose, put the dryer back in place, and restore power.

Clean your gas dryer.

Unfortunately, this isn't a job you can do yourself. Moving a gas dryer can rupture the gas line, which is not something you want to risk. Once a year, schedule a repairperson to inspect and clean your dryer.

Clean the dryer vent outlet.

Whether the dryer is gas or electric, you need to check the vent outlet every month or so. Pull out any lint and make sure the outlet isn't obstructed in any way.

All Other Appliances

Avoid ironing.

Yes, it's true: ironing is expensive. In fact, in an average family, an iron consumes as much energy as a clothes washer doing five loads of laundry a week. So, here's your official permission—no, make that encouragement—to avoid ironing whenever possible. You might even want to invest in some of those new, no-iron cottons that come out of the dryer ready to wear.

Insulate your waterbed.

Keeping a waterbed warm uses up a fair amount of energy in the winter, especially when you're trying to keep the house thermostat set low. Reduce the workload of your waterbed heater by insulating the bottom and sides of the mattress with foam insulating pads and covering the bed with a quilt to hold in the heat.

Unplug countertop appliances when you're not using them.

Toasters, curling irons, cell phone chargers, laptop chargers, and coffee pots draw electricity when they're plugged in, even if you're not using them. The average family can save $5 to $7 a month just by unplugging the countertop appliances they're not using.

Unplug small appliances and fixtures when you're away.

Before leaving for more than a couple of days, unplug all televisions, DVD players, computers, coffeepots, and so forth. Any device that displays or stores data is drawing electricity, even when you're not using it. Unplugging it while you're away takes very little time compared to the electricity it saves.

Run major appliances at night.

Appliances, such as the dishwasher, washer, and dryer, generate heat when they're operating. At any time of year, it's cheaper to run these appliances at night after the outdoor temperature has dropped. On a cool summer night, your air conditioner won't have to work as hard to overcome a running appliance as it would during the day. On a frigid winter night, the heat of a running appliance will give your heating system a boost.

Use cold water when you run the garbage disposal.

This tip saves energy and aggravation. Not only is cold water less expensive than hot water, but it prevents the kinds of grease clogs that hot water can create.

Chapter 4

Lighting

About 17 percent of the average household energy bill can be attributed to lighting. You can reduce your energy costs dramatically, by following these smart lighting tips.

Replace incandescent light bulbs with compact fluorescent lights.

Nothing will lower your energy costs as much as exchanging incandescent bulbs for compact fluorescent bulbs, or CFLs. CFLs cost more, but they use only 25 percent of the energy used by an incandescent bulb and last at least ten times longer. According to the Energy Information Administration, each CFL you install can save $30 to $60 over the life of the bulb.

QUICK TIP

Standard incandescent bulbs create more heat than light—up to 90 percent of the energy they use is given off as heat. When you're trying to cool your home, incandescent bulbs are actually working against you. Switch to CFLs and your cooling costs will go down along with your lighting costs.

CFLs are slightly larger than standard incandescent bulbs, so you may need to buy new harps, harp extenders, or adapters to help them fit into your lamps and fixtures. (A harp connects the shade to the lamp's socket.)

Replace outdoor lightbulbs with CFLs.

CFLs are now available for exterior light fixtures. These bulbs have to be placed in enclosed fixtures with cold-weather ballasts if they're used in extreme climates. If the bulb will be directly exposed to moisture, make sure it's labeled "wet location listed."

DETERMINING CFL REPLACEMENT BULB WATTAGE

CFLs produce the same amount of light at lower wattages than incandescent bulbs. To figure out the wattage necessary to replace an incandescent bulb, divide the wattage of the incandescent bulb by four. For example, a 60-watt incandescent bulb should be replaced with a 15-watt CFL.

Replace halogen floor lamps with CFL floor lamps.

Halogen floor lamps generate excessive heat, and some older models have even been proven to create fire hazards. Unfortunately, you can't exchange halogen bulbs for CFL bulbs. Instead, you'll need to replace halogen lamps with lamps designed for CFL bulbs. CFL compatible floor lamps are safer, plus they use 60 to 80 percent less energy.

Turn off the lights when you leave the room.

The simplest, and perhaps most cost-effective, energy-saving habit you can develop is to turn off lights, fixtures, and appliances when you're not using them. It may take a while, but if you can teach yourself to switch off the lights as you leave the room and turn off the television, radio, or computer when you're not using them, you'll save money and conserve energy.

Install motion-detector light fixtures.

Although leaving the outside light on for when you return is a good idea in terms of personal security, it's not a great way to save energy. You can have the security without the expense by replacing your outside lights with motion-detector fixtures that turn on as you approach. Follow these easy steps to install your new fixture: First, turn off the power to the circuit. Next, read every word of the instructions that came with the new fixture and prepare to follow them. Here are some basic directions:

Loosen the mounting screws on the old fixture and pull it loose from the wall. Then, check to make sure the power is off to the fixture. When you look at the back of the fixture, you'll find three sets of wires: one black, one white, and one green. Remove the wire caps connecting the fixture wires to the circuit wires coming from the wall. Use wire connectors to join the black wire on the new fixture to the black circuit wire; the white fixture wire to the white circuit wire; and the green fixture wire to the green circuit wire. To join the wires, strip half an inch of insulation from the ends, hold the wires parallel, insert them into the connector and twist it clockwise until the connector holds the wires snugly. Now, the only thing you have to do is remount the fixture. Check out the old mounting assembly. If it's compatible with the new fixture, simply put the mounting screws back in place. If not, replace the mounting assembly with the one provided with your motion-detector fixture.

Install a motion-detector switch in your walk-in closet.

Most of us rush through our daily routine, which makes it easy to forget to turn off the closet light as we streak toward the door. To fix this energy-draining problem, install a motion-detector switch on the closet light. Start by turning off the power to the circuit. Next, read every word of the instructions that came with the new switch and prepare to follow them. Generally speaking, what you're going to do is loosen the mounting screws on the old switch and pull it loose from the wall. Then, you're going to check to make sure the power is off to the circuit. Finally, you'll need to use wire connectors to connect the wire leads on the switch to the hot circuit wires. To join the wires, strip half an inch of insulation from the ends, hold the wires parallel, insert them into the connector and twist it clockwise until the connector holds them snugly.

Set a lamp on timer.

It's wonderful to come home to a lamp burning in the window, but it's unnecessarily expensive to leave a lamp on all day. Instead, buy an inexpensive timer and plug a lamp into it. Set the lamp to come on shortly before you get home from work and you'll come home to a well-lit room without the added expense.

Install touch lights under kitchen cabinets.

It's much more pleasant to work in a well-lit kitchen, but no one wants to spend a fortune upgrading their kitchen lighting. For a quick, energy-efficient solution, secure battery-operated touch lights to the bottoms of your kitchen cabinets using Velcro or double-sided foam tape.

Use task lighting.

Lighting designers say every room should include these light layers: ambient light (the light from windows and skylights), general lighting (often recessed lighting in the ceiling), task lighting (lamps and fixtures placed to illuminate specific activities), and accent lighting (light used for decorative purposes). While it's nice to have all of these elements, it's rarely necessary to use them all at once. Instead, use the fewest number of lights necessary for the task at hand. For example, turn off the overhead lights and turn on a reading lamp when you're about to enjoy your favorite book.

Position lamps for optimum lighting.

The bottom edge of a table-lamp shade should be at eye level when you're seated—about 38 to 42 inches above the floor. The bottom edge of a floor-lamp shade should be about 40 to 49 inches above the floor. Lamps used for reading should be positioned 15 inches to the side and 20 inches behind the center of the book as you're reading it.

Clean your light bulbs and fixtures.

Clean bulbs and fixtures are up to 100 percent more efficient than dusty ones. A couple quick fluffs with a feather duster will take care of most bulbs. Liquids don't mix with electricity, so avoid using liquid cleaners on bulbs or fixtures.

Chapter 5

Plumbing

Heating water accounts for about a third of the cost of maintaining a home. Conserving hot water in any way reduces your overall energy costs and eases the strain on your water supply.

Set the thermostat on your water heater to 120°F.

The ideal temperature to set your water heater is 120°F. That's hot enough to clean clothes and dishes efficiently and makes for comfortable showers and baths, but it's not hot enough to burn children and older people when it comes out of the tap. In most homes, you'll find the water heater in the mechanical area, near the furnace. A water heater is a large tank, often white or gray, with two water supply lines and an exhaust flue on top. On one side, near the bottom, you'll see a large label, a thermostat, and a dial. Before doing anything else, read the label for warnings and other important information. Adjust the temperature of your water by setting the dial to 120°F. If the dial is marked with words like "warm", "hot", "hotter" instead of numbers, check the owner's manual to see where to set it. Wait at least an hour and retest the water temperature.

To check the temperature of your water supply, let the hot water run for four or five minutes, then hold a candy thermometer in the stream for about a minute. Turn off the water and check the thermometer.

Flush the water heater.

Water heaters that gurgle and burp are calling for help! They're being choked by sediment, which makes them less efficient and can eventually clog the drain. To remove sediment, turn off the unit. If the heater is gas, set the gas valve to "pilot"; If it's electric, turn off the power to the circuit. Connect a hose to the spigot at the bottom of the tank. Put the other end of the hose in a sink or on a floor drain. Close the valve on the cold-water inlet, and pull up the lever on the pressure-relief valve. Turn on the spigot, but be careful—the water coming out will be hot! When the water runs clear, turn off the drain valve and remove the hose. Put the lever on the pressure-relief valve down and open the valve on the cold-water inlet. Elsewhere in the house, turn on a hot-water faucet (on the top floor, if you have more than one) and let the water run until it flows steadily, with no air bubbles. Turn the water heater back on.

QUICK TIP

To keep sediment from building up in the water heater, drain a gallon of water from it each month. This project only takes a few minutes, but it can prevent big problems from happening later.

Insulate your water heater.

Put your hand on the outside of your water heater. If it feels warm, installing an insulating blanket on the sides and top of the heater will help it retain more heat. If it feels cool, it's well insulated on the inside and doesn't need a blanket. NOTE: Always check the manufacturer's recommendations before insulating a gas water heater.

Turn off the water heater when you're away.

When you're away for four days or more, you save more by turning off the water heater than you spend heating the water from room temperature when you return. Before you leave for an extended absence, set the control on the water heater to **OFF END**.

Insulate water pipes.

Hot water loses heat as it travels from the water heater to the faucet. Insulating the water pipes can reduce energy costs, especially if the pipes run through unheated spaces, like crawl spaces. Purchase sleeve-type foam insulation at your local hardware store or home center. Close off the hot water supply and wait for the pipes to cool before insulating them. The foam sleeves are slit lengthwise, so all you have to do is open the tube and fit it around the pipe. Be sure to cover at least the first ten feet of the hot- and cold-water pipes leaving the water heater and all pipes running through uninsulated spaces.

Take showers rather than baths.

Most of us love baths, but they use up a lot of hot water: An average tub bath uses more than twice as much hot water as a seven-minute shower. With this in mind, savor a long, luxurious bath from time to time, but use the shower when it comes to your daily routine.

Turn up the water heater before filling a tub.

To cut down on the cost of bathing in a tub, turn up the thermostat on the water heater to 140°F about an hour before you start filling it. Start with a tub full of room temperature water and then add just enough 140°F water to make it comfortable. As soon as you finish your bath, turn the water heater's thermostat back to 120°F.

Install a low-flow showerhead.

Today's low-flow showerheads deliver invigorating showers despite their hot-water-saving, penny-pinching ways. A low-flow showerhead can save $10 to $20 per person every year, and installing one is a breeze. Simply grasp the neck of the old showerhead with an adjustable wrench, and turn until the showerhead comes off. Wrap Teflon tape around the threads of the pipe sticking out of the shower wall, and then thread the new showerhead onto it. Wrap the jaws of the wrench with masking tape to keep it from scratching the new showerhead, and then use the wrench to tighten the showerhead onto the pipe.

ENERGY SAVER ALERT

Showerheads manufactured after 1994 must use 2.5 gallons of water or less per minute to meet improved national water efficiency standards. Older showerheads may use more than twice that amount! If you're not sure how old your showerhead is, don't fret: It's easy to find out whether it wastes hot water. Get a watch or clock with a second hand and an empty half-gallon milk carton. Hold the milk carton in front of the showerhead, turn on the water, and watch the clock. If it takes less than ten seconds to fill the carton, you could save money by installing a low-flow showerhead.

Install a faucet aerator.

Without an aerator, hot water gushes out of a sink faucet. With one, the flow is reduced to 2.2 gallons per minute, and you save money. An aerator simply screws onto the end of the faucet. Kitchen sink fixtures can even be fitted with a dual-flow aerator that produces either a single or shower-type stream.

QUICK TIP

Before you go shopping for an aerator, remove the existing cap on your faucet (and bring it with you to the store) or leave it on and measure it carefully. When you get to the plumbing aisle of your favorite home center or hardware store, compare the aerators to the dimensions of your faucet to ensure compatibility.

Adjust the sink stopper so the sink holds water.

Almost every list of water-saving habits includes the idea that you should fill the sink rather than running the water when you do things like shave. It's a good, money-saving idea, as long as the sink holds water. If the water disappears down the drain before you finish shaving, you'll have to run it more despite your good intentions. Good news: In less than ten minutes, you can adjust the stopper so the sink holds water. First, adjust the lift rod, the rod you pull up and push down to open and close the stopper. It's attached to the back of a metal clevis strap and held in place with a screw. Turn the screw counterclockwise, and adjust the lift rod until the stopper is closed when the lever is all the way up. Tighten the screw and test the stopper. If the screw is stuck, spray it with lubricating spray and let it sit for a few minutes. If the sink stopper has lost its pop, adjust the pivot rod. Under the sink, you'll see a small metal pivot rod that extends from the drain pipe into a hole in the metal clevis strap. To adjust the pivot rod, pinch the V-shaped spring clip and pull off the rod. Move it into a different hole in the clevis strap, replace the spring clip and test the drain.

Replace your pop-up sink stopper.

If adjusting the pivot rod and lift rod doesn't help you keep water in the sink, it's time to replace the whole darn thing. This sounds complicated, but I promise it's not. All you have to do is loosen the nut holding the pivot rod into the drainpipe and the screw holding the lift rod into the clevis strap, and remove the mechanism. Take it to a hardware store or home center and buy a replacement. Thread the lift rod into the clevis strap and tighten the screw; insert the ball-end of the pivot rod into the drainpipe and tighten the nut. Set and adjust the pivot rod in the clevis strap. You're finished!

Fix leaky faucets.

Faucet leaks are expensive: A fast drip can waste as much as 429 gallons of water and 107 kilowatt hours every month if you have an electric water heater. A leaky faucet is easy enough to fix if you take your time and pay attention to how the parts are positioned as you take them apart. If you're nervous about getting it all back together, label the parts and draw diagrams or take digital or instant pictures as you go.

To fix a leaky faucet, you have to know what type of faucet you have and where the leak originates. On the following pages I will explain how to fix four of the most common types of household faucets.

Ball faucet—Beneath the single handle of a ball faucet, a hollow metal or plastic ball controls the temperature and flow of water. If a ball faucet leaks from the spout, grip the knurled edges of the faucet cap with slip-joint pliers and tighten the cap. If that doesn't stop the leak, turn off the water at the shut-off valves, and take the faucet apart. Use an Allen wrench to loosen the setscrew, then lift off the handle. Grip the faucet cap with your slip-joint pliers and remove it. Make sure your sink drain is closed before you start taking out the small parts. Next, lift out the cam, cam washer, and ball. With a small screwdriver, pry out the springs and the valve seats. Take these parts to a hardware or home center so you can identify the right replacement parts. Reassemble the faucet with the new parts, and the leak should be gone.

When a ball-type faucet leaks from the base, you'll need to replace the O-rings. Turn off the shut-off valves and remove the handle. Next, twist the spout up and off to remove it, then cut off the old O-rings. Coat new O-rings with heatproof grease and put them in place. Press the spout down until its collar settles on the plastic slip ring, then put the handle assembly back together. Turn the faucet on and gradually open the shutoff valves, watching for leaks. Tighten the connections, if necessary.

Cartridge faucet—If you take the handle off and find a cartridge and movable stem, you've got a cartridge faucet. Worn seals are the cause of most spout leaks on these faucets, and the best thing to do is to replace the cartridge. Turn off the water at the shutoff valves, then pry off the index cap and remove the screw in the center of the faucet handle. Lift the handle up and tilt it backward to get it off. The next thing you'll come to is a plastic retaining ring—use slip-joint pliers to turn it counterclockwise and remove it. If there is a retaining clip holding the cartridge in place, remove it. Now we've come to the good part: Grip the cartridge with your slip-joint pliers and pull straight up. Take the cartridge to the store and find a replacement. Reverse this process to install the new cartridge. Make sure the cartridge is lined up just like the old one, with the tab facing forward.

Most leaks from a base are caused by worn out O-rings. Remove the handle as described above, and then pull up and twist the spout to remove it. Cut the old O-rings and remove them. Coat the new O-rings with heatproof grease and install them. Reassemble the spout and faucet, then turn the faucet on and gradually open the shutoff valves. Check for leaks and tighten connections as necessary.

Disc-type faucet—Disc faucets have a single handle and a wide cylinder inside. Whether they come from the spout or around the body, most leaks are caused by dirty seals or cylinder openings. To fix them, turn off the water at the shutoff valves. Turn the faucet spout to the side, then lift the handle. Remove the setscrew and lift off the handle and cap. Several screws hold the cylinder in place: remove them and lift out the cylinder. If it looks worn, take it to the store and buy a new one. If it looks okay, carefully remove the seals from the cylinder openings, then use a scrubbie pad to clean the openings and inlet holes. Rinse the cylinder. Replace the seals and put the faucet back together. Turn the handle to **ON END** and very gradually open the shutoff valves until the water runs steadily, with no bursts of air.

Compression faucet —A faucet with separate handles for hot and cold water and a threaded stem assembly inside the body is a compression faucet. When one of these begins to leak, it's probably time to have it replaced by a professional plumber. The number and placement of holes in the sink will dictate the type of replacement faucet you choose to some extent, so consult with the plumber before choosing one.

Repair a leaky hose bib.

Hose bibs—faucets with threaded spouts that can be connected to utility or appliance hoses—leak when the washers or seals wear out. Don't let water go to waste when you can fix the leak in just a few steps. The replacement parts you need can be found in universal washer kits at hardware stores and home centers. When you're ready to begin your repair, take a look at the handle on top of the faucet. You'll see a screw in the center of the handle. Loosen and remove that screw, then lift off the handle. Now, you'll see a large nut right above the faucet. With the handle off, you'll be able to loosen that nut with an adjustable wrench, and then remove the nut and the washer beneath it. Next, unscrew and remove the spindle, the stem that reaches down into the faucet. If you can't turn it by hand, use an adjustable wrench. Cover the jaws of the wrench with masking tape first, and be careful not to damage the spindle. Turn the spindle upside down and remove the stem screw and washer. Coat the new stem washer and packing washer with heatproof grease, and reverse this process to put the hose bib back together.

QUICK TIP

According to the American Water Works Association, up to 14 percent of the water consumed in a home is wasted through plumbing leaks. Finding and fixing those leaks saves money on your water bills as well as your energy bills.

PART TWO

Heating, Ventilation, and Air Conditioning Advice

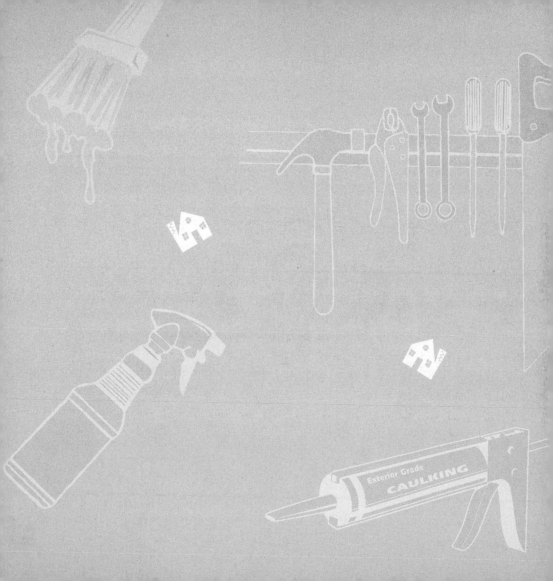

Chapter 6

Heating

While producing heat efficiently within your home should be one of your energy-saving goals, making sure your home retains heat is equally important. The tips in this chapter will help you to accomplish both.

Install a programmable thermostat.

A programmable thermostat automatically adjusts the temperature according to the settings you've programmed. Setting the temperature back just 10°F for eight hours at night and another eight hours during the day while you're at work can cut your energy bills by 20 percent. Best of all, installing a thermostat is a snap. Before you start, read the instructions that accompany your new thermostat and prepare to follow them exactly. In general, you can expect to start by turning off the power to your heating and cooling system at the main service panel. Next, you'll need to remove the cover plate on the old thermostat, loosen the screw terminals and disconnect the wires. Some thermostats come with labels you can use to mark the low voltage wires to identify their screw-terminal locations. If the model you've chosen doesn't include labels, you can use masking tape to mark the wires. Either way, you need to label the wires so you'll know where to connect them on the new thermostat. After the wires are labeled, unscrew the mounting screws and pull off the thermostat body. With the old body out of the way, you can thread the low-voltage wires through the base of the new thermostat, and then mount the base on the wall. (Thermostats need to be level, so you'll need to check it with a level to make sure you've gotten it properly positioned.) Now, you can connect the low-voltage wires to the screw terminals on the base, following the labels you added earlier. With the wires in place, install the batteries in the thermostat body and then attach the body to the thermostat base. Finally, all that remains is to restore the power to the heating and cooling system at the main service panel and program the thermostat as directed by the manufacturer's instructions.

Change your furnace filter.

A furnace filter cleans air on the way into the system, before dust, pollen, and other airborne particles can be recirculated. To keep your furnace performing at its best, be sure to change the filter every month during heating season. To do so, check the area between the furnace and the cold air duct for the old filter or filter compartment. If you don't see the filter immediately, check the owner's manual for the exact location—you may have to remove an access cover to get to it. Grasp the old filter and pull it out, being careful not to get it caught on the sides of the blower housing. Hold the new filter so the arrow on top is pointing in the direction of airflow (from the cold air duct toward the furnace) and slide it into place. That's all there is to it!

Some thermostats signal when the furnace filter needs to be replaced. If you have trouble remembering to replace the filter, install a programmable thermostat with this feature.

Clean the air intake and exhaust on your forced-air heating system.

On an outside wall of the house, you'll find an air intake and exhaust. It's critical to keep the areas around the intake and exhaust free and clear. Every month or so during the heating season, remove snow, leaves and other debris and prune any plants or bushes that might interfere with airflow.

Clean your electronic air filter.

If your heating system includes a built-in electronic air filter, it will need to be cleaned every month to keep air flowing efficiently into the furnace. Remove the filter and use cool water and a soft brush to scrub it clean or run it through the dishwasher on a light, gentle cycle. Do not use the dry cycle. Let the filter air dry before you replace it.

QUICK TIP

Standard furnace filters work adequately, but pleated filters and electrically charged filters remove finer dust and can be cleaned and reused rather than discarded.

Clean all cold-air returns.

Forced-air furnaces require a constant flow of air, and cold-air returns are a big part of that flow. Look around any room in the house. You should see a large register cover somewhere on a wall, 6 or 8 inches from the floor. That's a cold-air return. Keep your cold-air returns clean and make sure they're not blocked by furniture or draperies.

Clean all heat registers.

If you have a forced-air heating system, every room in your house has heat registers, small vents through which the heat flows into the room. Heat registers are usually in or near the floor, and there's almost always one near every window and door. At the beginning and end of the heating season, pull off each register cover and vacuum the cover itself. Next, reach down into the heat duct and clean it as far back as possible. Replace the register covers and your job is done.

ENERGY SAVER ALERT

When you first discover heat register filters at your local hardware store or home center, they may seem like a good idea. After all, adding more filters will keep more dust and dirt out of the house, right? Not so fast! Anything that restricts airflow through the system reduces its efficiency and costs you money. Less dust is a good thing, but how much do you want to pay for that convenience? These filters are rarely worth the increase in your energy bills.

Schedule a tune-up for your furnace.

Just like a car, a furnace works most efficiently when its working parts are in tip-top condition. Have new furnaces checked and tuned up every two to three years; older systems should be tuned up at least every other year. Many utility companies offer this service at reasonable prices. Be sure you're getting an actual cleaning and tune-up, not just a safety check. The process should take between two to three hours and cost between $100 to $150, depending on where you live.

Seal heat ducts.

Large metal ducts carry warm and cool air throughout the house, delivering it to individual rooms. These ducts have seams, and those seams leak air if they're not sealed. In areas where the ducts are exposed, such as those with unfinished or suspended ceilings, you can seal the seams in a heat duct in under ten minutes, using hybrid tape that combines a thin layer of putty with an aluminum foil facing or pure silicone caulk. Pay special attention to the areas near the furnace, especially the joints between the duct and the furnace itself.

Seal the joints between heat ducts and heat registers.

Heat ducts run through cavities in the floors, ending at the heat registers. Warm air can leak between the edges of the duct and the floor if those edges aren't sealed. Again, this is easy to fix. Pull off the register cover and use hybrid duct-sealing tape to seal the edges of the duct to the edges of the floor.

If, like me, you grew up believing you can do anything with duct tape, this might shock you: Duct tape is great for everything except sealing ducts. Duct tape will come apart within a few years, and you'll have to go through the whole process again. Other tapes create a more permanent seal, which saves both time and money. Look for special tape that carries the Underwriter's Laboratories logo, a symbol that indicates the tape meets or exceeds recognized performance standards.

Move items that block air circulation.

Warm air works most efficiently when it can circulate freely. Keep furniture, draperies and other items away from heat registers and radiators.

You know it's important to keep the heat registers clear, but what if one of your most beloved window treatments blocks a heat register? Instead of taking the draperies down, get an inexpensive deflector for the register and direct the warm air down and out from under the window treatments. (Remember, heat rises, so directing the heat down improves circulation.) You'll find deflectors near the replacement furnace filters in your local home center or hardware store.

Control the flow of heat.

Every heat register cover has a device used to open or close the vents behind the fins. Some have a dial and others have a knob, but they all have some way to control the flow of heat through the register. Open the vents to introduce more heat into the room; close them to limit the heat. Because heat rises, you may want to close the vents on upper floors and open them on lower floors to direct more heat to colder areas.

Clean your radiators.

A clean radiator is an efficient radiator; so clean yours at least once a month. Close the valve and let the radiator cool, then use the brush tool on your vacuum cleaner to dust the surface and a lamb's wool duster to clean between the fins. After dusting, wash it with warm water and a little detergent.

Refinish your radiators.

Too many layers of paint reduce a radiator's efficiency. If your radiators are clogged with paint, strip and refinish them.

QUICK TIP

To increase the amount of heat a radiator puts out, paint it a dark color, and then place a piece of aluminum or sheet metal behind it.

Keep your sense of humidity.

My grandmother always said it wasn't the heat that made the southern Missouri summers miserable, it was the humidity. She was right: Because water is such a good conductor of heat, humid air feels warmer. By keeping the air at a comfortable humidity level, you can keep the thermostat turned down low and still feel comfortably warm. Running a humidifier, some living plants to your home, or leave the exhaust fan off while you shower once in a while.

QUICK TIP

It's easy to find out if you need to add humidity to the air in your house. Take a glass and three ice cubes into a bedroom or living room—any room other than a kitchen or bathroom. Wait three minutes. If water beads up on the outside of the glass, the humidity level is fine. If not, the air is too dry.

The human body is most comfortable when the relative humidity is between 20 and 60 percent. According to the Minnesota Blue Flame Gas Association, a relative humidity of 35 to 40 percent is appropriate inside your home when the outdoor temperature is above 20°F.

Caulk gaps between the floor and the baseboard.

On hard floors, such as vinyl or hardwood, the baseboards are often finished out with quarter-round trim. If there are large gaps between the baseboard and the floor or the baseboard and the quarter round, you've got air leaks. You can either caulk the gaps or, depending on how large the gaps actually are, pull off the quarter round, fill the gap with expandable foam, then replace the trim.

Insulate outlets and switches on exterior walls.

Switch and outlet boxes are set into wall cavities, which means they can leak air, especially when they're located on exterior walls. Next time you're at a hardware store or home center, pick up some insulating gaskets and get ready to fix this problem. Simply remove the screw that holds the cover to the box, press the gasket in place around the switch or receptacle, and replace the cover. You should be able to do several rooms in ten minutes, and the whole house in less than an hour.

Close off unused rooms.

There's no need to heat rooms you never use. Close the doors to unused rooms and cover the heat registers with magnetic vent covers.

Add glass doors to your wood-burning fireplace.

Wood-burning fireplaces are romantic and beautiful, but they're not energy efficient. An open flue—even with a fire burning—is a giant hole, sucking warmth from the house. One way to limit the heat loss of a wood-burning fireplace is to have glass doors installed over the fireplace. This is a critical energy-saving step. Even if you hire someone to do this for you, it won't take long for your energy savings to pay back your investment.

Close the damper on a wood-burning fireplace.

An open fireplace damper loses as much heat as a four-foot hole in an exterior wall of your house. As soon as the fire is completely out, close the damper on the fireplace. Do this every single time you have a fire. No exceptions.

Convert a wood-burning fireplace to gas.

When you convert a wood-burning fireplace to gas, you have two choices: buying a vented gas log or a vent-free gas log. Before making this decision, research the products you are considering and talk with your utility provider or an HVAC expert about their recommendations for your specific climate and home. Once you've decided on a product, hire a professional to run a gas line to your fireplace and help you install the log. If you choose a vent-free gas log, seal the fireplace flue before installing the log.

ENERGY SAVER ALERT

Vent-free gas logs may seem like a bad idea to those of us who make sure that every combustion device in the home is well vented, but improvements in technology are challenging this notion. The new vent-free gas logs are 99 percent efficient, which means that 99 percent of the gases produced are burned in the process rather than emitted into your home. In fact, some experts believe that vent-free logs produce fewer emissions than vented gas logs.

Install a vent-free gas log and fireplace.

Santa Clause may beg to differ, but with the advent of vent-free gas logs, it's no longer necessary to have a chimney in order to have a fireplace. Simply buy a fireplace surround and a vent-free gas log at your local home center, hire a professional to extend the gas line, set up the rest, and you're ready to gather round the hearth on winter evenings.

Adjust the air shutter on a vented gas fireplace.

The flames in a vented gas fireplace should be blue with yellowish tips. If the flames in your fireplace don't look like that, adjust the primary air shutter, which you should find on the control panel. If that doesn't fix the problem, call a fireplace specialist. Don't take any chances on this—a poorly adjusted gas fireplace wastes energy and can be a serious health hazard.

Turn off the gas fireplace when you're not in the room.

Depending on the region where you live, the company that provides your utilities, and the size of the unit, the cost of burning a natural gas fireplace is between 22¢ and 55¢ an hour (based on the anticipated cost of natural gas during the 2005-2006 heating season). You may feel that the romance and warmth of the fire are worth that price when you're snuggled around the hearth, but it's a lot to pay for a fire you're not there to enjoy. If your fireplace is controlled by a switch or a remote control, develop the habit of turning it off when you leave the room.

Adjust the flames on a gas fireplace.

It's common sense: smaller flames consume less gas. On the control panel of your gas fireplace, you should find a knob with markings that indicate **HIGH END** and **LOW END** and a range in between. Dial down the flames and you'll dial down the cost of running the fireplace, too.

Play the zone.

Zone heating is a concept that involves turning the main heating system down to 55°F and using supplemental heaters only in the room or rooms you're using at any given moment. If you decide to try this concept, set the supplemental heaters at the lowest setting that's comfortable for you. Remember to unplug them—don't just turn them off, unplug them—when they're not being used.

Choose and use space heaters wisely.

Space heaters make sense when you're trying to keep heating costs down, but some can be dangerous. Buy them wisely and use them carefully. Radiant heaters are the most efficient type of space heat, and the best ones power down when the room reaches the desired temperature. Always keep fabric, paper, and other combustible materials well away from space heaters, and unplug them when you're not using them.

Clean your baseboard heaters.

A dirty baseboard heater doesn't keep a room as warm as a clean one. To clean a baseboard heater, turn off the power and use a neon tester to make sure the power is off. Remove the front panel and use the crevice tool on a vacuum cleaner to remove dust and dirt from the element. If any of the metal fins are badly bent, use a pair of needle nose pliers to straighten them. (Don't worry about slightly bent fins—they don't hurt a thing.) Replace the cover and restore the power.

Adjust your ceiling fan.

Ceiling fans adjusted to turn clockwise during the heating season will effectively push warm air down into the room. Turn the fan on and watch which direction the blades turn. If they're turning counterclockwise, turn the fan off and get out a stepladder. Look for an adjustment switch on the head at the center of the fan. Slide it in the opposite direction, and then move yourself and the ladder out of the way. Turn the fan on and make sure the blades are moving clockwise.

Use portable fans to distribute warm air.

In rooms without ceiling fans, small portable fans are remarkably effective at distributing warm air, especially in rooms that have fireplaces. My mom and dad taught me this one: They keep a small fan on the hearth in front of their fireplace, pointed toward the ceiling. The air from the fan pushes warm air down from the ceiling and mixes it with the cooler air below. By running that little fan, they distribute heat from the fireplace throughout the main floor of their house.

Cover your window air conditioning unit.

Setting up a window air conditioner is an aggravating project, which means that most people leave theirs in place year round. While this may be more convenient, it also allows air to seep in and out around the unit. Prevent this problem by placing a window-air-conditioner cover over the back of your air conditioner. Securely tape a piece of sheet plastic over the front of the unit, and you'll keep your money from flying out the window.

Replace a standard bathroom bulb with a heat bulb.

Turning down the thermostat isn't much of a problem when you're dressed for cool temperatures, but what about when you're not dressed at all? Most of us hate to be greeted by cold air when we step out of the shower or bath. To solve this problem without having to turn up the thermostat, buy a red moisture-resistant heat bulb in a wattage that matches the wattage of your fixture. Install the bulb in a fixture near the shower or tub and enjoy instant, low-cost warmth.

Maintain the condenser unit on a heat pump.

A heat pump's condenser unit needs to be clean to work efficiently. To do so, shut off the power at the unit's disconnect switch and at the main service panel. When you're sure the power is off, remove the access panels. Next, put on heavy gloves and remove any debris from around the condenser coil, fan, and motor. With a garden hose and a soft-bristle brush, wash the outer fins and coils. Use a fin comb with appropriately sized teeth to straighten any fins that are bent. Finally, turn the fan and watch whether it rotates smoothly. If not, tighten the screws holding the blades to the brackets. If a blade is bent, have a professional replace the fan assembly.

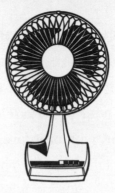

Chapter 7

Ventilation

Good ventilation is essential to a healthy, comfortable home. Maintaining proper humidity levels helps keep you warm at lower temperatures and cool at higher temperatures, which saves energy and money.

Turn off exhaust fans once they've cleared the air.

Exhaust fans recycle the air in a room, which means they remove the conditioned air and replace it with fresh air, as often as eight times an hour in the case of bathroom fans. If your home has problems with moisture, using an exhaust fan while bathing or cooking is essential. The trouble is, during heating and cooling season when you're paying to condition the air, removing it is an expensive proposition. Run the fan while you cook and bathe, but turn it off as soon as the moisture is cleared, typically about twenty minutes.

Install a timer switch for your exhaust fan.

If you have a hard time remembering to turn off the bathroom exhaust fan, replace the regular switch with a timer switch. To install a timer switch, first turn off the power to the circuit. Next, read every word of the instructions that came with the new switch and prepare to follow them. Generally speaking, you'll need to loosen the mounting screws on the old switch and pull it loose from the wall. Then, you're going to check to make sure the power is off to the circuit. Finally, you'll need to use wire connectors to connect the wire leads on the switch to the hot circuit wires. To join the wires, strip half an inch of insulation from the ends, hold the wires parallel, insert them into the connector and twist it clockwise until the connector holds the wires snugly. Now you can set the timer and go!

Close foundation vents during the heating season.

Foundations over crawlspaces have vents designed to provide fresh air to that space. This ventilation is absolutely necessary during warm, humid weather, but it's unnecessary and expensive to let cold air circulate beneath your living space in the winter. Close or block your foundation vents during heating season, but be absolutely sure you open them again in the spring. NOTE: Not every house has a crawlspace, an unexcavated area beneath the foundation of a house. They're common in some regions and almost unheard of in others. If you have one, you probably are quite aware of it. If you've never heard of one, it's unlikely that your house has one.

It's critical to reopen foundation vents in the spring. Without ventilation, moisture could build up in the crawl-space and lead to mold, mildew, and other nasty problems. If you're not absolutely sure you'll remember, make a note on your calendar, put it in your date book, or set an alarm in your PDA.

Maintain your air-to-air exchanger.

Air-to-air exchangers are the HVAC industry's answer to the lack of fresh air in today's super-insulated homes. Most new homes have an exchanger—in some communities, buildings codes even require them. If you have one, you'll find it near the furnace. One large duct runs from the exchanger, housed in a metal box, to an outside wall and another duct runs to the furnace. Like most air-handling equipment, exchangers have filters that need to be cleaned periodically. Depending on the manufacturer's recommendations, you should clean your air filter every one to three months. Remove the cover and take out washable filters; clean them with mild soap and water. Let the filters dry completely before you put them back. Replace disposable filters. Next, clean the heat recovery core, which transfers heat from indoor air to the fresh air coming into the heating system. To clean the core, remove the cover of the exchanger and slide out the metal rods that hold it in place.

Clean the core with cool water and mild detergent, and then rinse it thoroughly. Let the core dry thoroughly before you replace it. Finally, look for the air intake screen. A duct connects the air-to-air exchanger to an air intake on an exterior wall of the house. Follow the duct from the unit to a wall, and you'll find this screen on the outside. Remove any dirt, debris, animal nests, or plants you find on the screen. In the winter, check the screen frequently to make sure it isn't frozen over.

Increase ventilation in your attic.

If your attic doesn't have enough ventilation, truly unpleasant problems can develop, such as ice dams in the winter and moisture problems in the summer. When heat builds up in your attic during the summer, you also have to pay more to keep your house cool. Here's an easy way to find out if you attic needs more vents: Measure the attic's existing openings and then check the floor plans to find the room's square footage. The house should have at least 1 square foot of vent openings for every 300 square feet of attic floor space. If your ventilation doesn't meet this standard or if you have questions about attic ventilation, consult a qualified building contractor.

Chapter 8

Cooling

There are plenty of more affordable ways to keep your house cool than running an air conditioner day and night. Read on for some alternative cooling tips.

Block out the sun.

Blinds and shades block the sun and keep it from heating up your rooms. Opaque roller shades block 80 percent of the heat gain that occurs through uncovered windows, and white Venetian blinds block 45 to 50 percent.

Use a window fan at night.

Summer evenings are often cool enough that you can turn off your air conditioner and rely on a window fan. Place the fan in the window to draw indoor air outside, and, if possible, open a window in an opposite room to create a pleasant cross breeze.

Use fans as often as possible. With just a 2-miles-per-hour breeze, you feel as cool at 82°F as you would at 78°F with no breeze.

Use a ceiling fan to help cool air rise.

Ceiling fans adjusted to turn counterclockwise push cool air up off the floor. Turn the fan on and watch which direction the blades turn. If they're turning clockwise, turn the fan off and get out a stepladder. Find the adjustment switch on the head at the center of the fan. Slide it in the opposite direction, and then move yourself and the ladder out of the way. Turn the fan on and make sure the blades are moving counterclockwise.

Direct cool air upward from the registers.

It's a law of nature: warm air rises and cool air sinks. And, just as warm air doesn't offer much comfort when it's floating on the ceiling, cool air doesn't help when it's lurking around your ankles. No problem. The same deflectors that direct air down toward the floor during heating season can be used to direct cool air up from the registers during the cooling season. Simply reverse the vent and you're ready for summer.

Don't cool the air when you're not home.

When you leave home for more than four hours, set the thermostat up to 85° F. You'll save more energy by doing this than it will take to cool the house when you return.

Help your thermostat get an accurate reading.

Fixtures and appliances, such as televisions and lamps, can give off enough heat to make the thermostat call for more cooling cycles than are truly necessary. Keeping these devices away from your thermostat helps keep cooling costs down.

Clean and maintain your air conditioner's condenser unit.

The condenser unit—the part of the air conditioner that sits outside—needs to be clean to work efficiently. Shut off the power at the unit's disconnect switch and at the main service panel. When you're sure the power is off, remove the access panels. Wearing heavy gloves, remove any debris from around the condenser coil, fan, and motor. Use a garden hose and a soft-bristle brush to wash the outer fins and coils. Draw a fin comb along the fins to straighten any that are bent. Turn the fan and watch whether it rotates smoothly. If not, tighten the screws holding the blades to the brackets. If a blade is bent, have a professional replace the fan assembly.

Turn off the pilot light on a gas fireplace.

The pilot light on a gas fireplace puts out a surprising amount of heat. There are pros and cons to turning off the pilot light during the cooling season. On the positive side, you won't be burning natural gas or running the air conditioner to combat the heat produced by the pilot light if you turn it off. On the other hand, some manufacturers claim that moisture can build up and spiders and mites can nest in the lines if you turn off the pilot light. Check your owner's manual or consult your natural gas supplier and decide what's best for your specific circumstances. If you decide to turn off the pilot light, follow the manufacturer's instructions to the letter. You can expect to be directed to close down the gas supply and then turn the control knob to **OFF END**. When it's time to relight the pilot, you have to remove the glass front on the fireplace, turn on the gas supply, turn the control knob to **PILOT END**, push the ignition button until the flame ignites, and then replace the glass.

QUICK TIP

Most manufacturers of gas fireplaces recommend a check-up and cleaning at the beginning of every heating season. If you decide to turn off the pilot light for the cooling season, you could have the serviceperson relight it during this seasonal check-up.

Put a timer on your window air conditioner.

There's no reason to leave a window air conditioner running all day if you're not home to enjoy the cool air. There's no reason to come home to an uncomfortable room, either. Instead, plug the air conditioner into an inexpensive timer and set it to turn on half an hour before you get home.

Maintain a room air conditioner.

Keep your air conditioner working efficiently by cleaning it every so often. Unplug the unit and remove the access cover on the front. Pull out the filter and wash it with water and a mild detergent. Let the filter dry thoroughly before you put it back inside. Remove the back panel and vacuum the condenser fins using the brush tool on a vacuum cleaner. Use a fin comb to straighten any bent fins, then replace the back cover. Now look at the back of the unit: You should find a drain hole and a drain pan just below the condenser coils. Soak up any water in the pan with a sponge or rag; inspect and clean the drain hole. Wash the drain pan with equal parts of bleach and water. When you're finished, reinstall the unit.

Close the registers in the basement.

Basements are, by their very nature, at least partially surrounded by soil, which keeps them naturally cool. Closing the register vents to the basement makes more cool air available to the rest of the house. To close the registers, simply pull the knob or adjust the dial to close the louvers beneath the cover.

Replace or clean the furnace filter every month.

Air flows through your heating system on its way into your central air conditioning system, so it's just as important to change the furnace filters during cooling season as it is to change them during heating season. Changing the filter is simple: As you approach the furnace, look between it and the cold air duct for the old filter or filter compartment. If you don't see the filter immediately, check the owner's manual for the exact location. (You may have to remove an access cover to get to the filter.) Grasp the old filter and pull it out, being careful not to let it catch on the sides of the blower housing. Hold the new filter so the arrow on top is pointing in the direction of airflow—from the cold air duct toward the furnace—and slide it into place. That's all there is to it!

Clean electrostatic filters every month.

If your system includes an electronic air filter, you need to wash the filter every month during cooling season. Use cool water and a soft scrub brush or run the filter through a light, gentle cycle in the dishwasher. Don't use the dry cycle. Let the filters air dry, then replace them.

Recharge and recycle your air conditioning refrigerant.

Hire an HVAC professional to recharge and recycle the refrigerant in your air conditioning system every two years.

Turn off your humidifier.

Ask anyone—humid air feels warmer than dry air. That's a good thing in the winter, but not in the summer. If you have a central humidifier system on your furnace, turn it off during the cooling season. You'll save the energy it uses and—more importantly—you'll be comfortable at higher temperatures, which means the air conditioner won't have to run as often.

Run a dehumidifier during humid weather.

When it's hot and humid, run a dehumidifier. With less moisture in the air, you can set the thermostat higher and still be comfortable.

PART THREE

Outdoor Savings

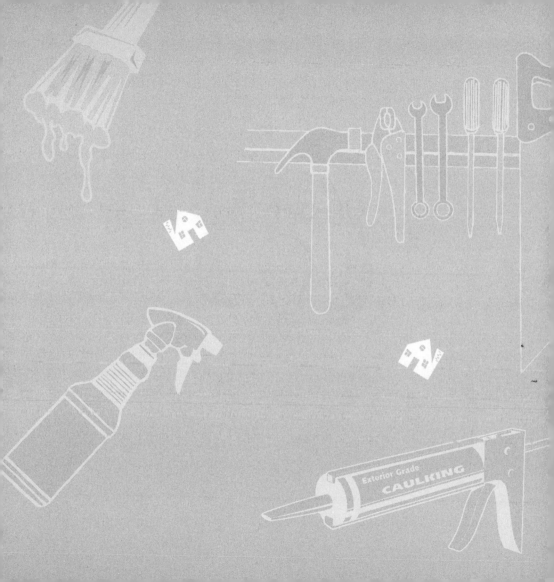

Chapter 9

Outdoors

From caulking your siding to landscaping with energy in mind, the great outdoors holds all sorts of possibilities for saving energy.

Plant some shade.

Plant trees and shrubs on the west and south sides of your house to shade your home and keep it cool. Deciduous, or leaf-shedding, trees are best because they become bare in the winter when you want the sun to shine through and warm your home. With just one tree shading your walls and roof during the afternoon, you can reduce wall and roof temperatures by 20 to 40°F. When the walls and roof are cooler, less hot air finds its way into the house, and the air conditioner runs less often.

Install awnings, arbors, and pergolas.

Any device that shades your windows, especially on the south and west sides of the house, reduces solar gain through the windows. If you install awnings, choose models that can be removed or retracted easily in the winter. If you build an arbor or pergola, plant trailing and creeping vines to cover it with beautiful color and add more cooling shade.

Plant natural insulation.

Vines and shrubs growing next to the house create air spaces that help keep the house cool in the summer and warm in the winter. Install a trellis and train some vines and trailing plants to grow up it. NOTE: Don't train vines to grow directly on the house. Vines can damage the siding with their tendrils and suckers.

Provide shade for skylights.

Plant large trees to shade skylights. These days, you don't have to wait quite as long for trees to grow—a qualified arborist with the right equipment can plant mature trees successfully. Of course, large trees are expensive, but so is cooling a room with an unshaded skylight. Talk with a local nursery and your utility company, and find out how long it will take for the energy savings to equal the investment.

Plant shade for driveways, sidewalks, and patios.

Anyone who has ever played on an asphalt driveway or playground knows how hot it can get, and concrete isn't much better. Around your house, the heat from the driveway and sidewalks radiates up to the walls of the house and heats it up. Shading these surfaces reduces the amount of heat they reflect toward your house. Adding trees, shrubs, plants, and flowers along the sides of your driveway and walkway improves the curb appeal of your home and reduces your energy costs. Quite a trick for such a small investment of time and money!

Plant evergreen trees on the north and northwest sides of the house.

Drive through the farmlands of Iowa, and you'll see evergreen windbreaks on the north side of nearly every homestead. In some places, if it weren't for those trees, there wouldn't be a thing to break the wind for miles and miles. Although the situation at your house isn't likely to be as drastic, a row of evergreens to the north of the house will block winter winds and prevent drafts.

Caulk around vents and other fittings.

Apply silicone caulk around dryer vents, exhaust fan vents, and other fittings mounted on the siding of your house. If you find old caulk there already, remove it completely before adding new caulk.

Add caulk wherever two dissimilar materials meet.

It's a simple theory: There are bound to be gaps wherever two dissimilar materials meet, and those gaps leak air. Fortunately, a few minutes with a caulk gun will take care of those leaks for good.

Learn how to caulk like a pro.

The more skilled you are in caulking, the more energy you will save. Make sure you know how to do it right before you begin.

For exterior caulking, all you need is a caulking gun with a racheted plunger. To load the gun, pull back on the plunger and drop the new tube of caulk in the barrel, back end first. Pull the trigger or push the plunger until it reaches the back of the caulk cartridge. Next, cut off the end of the nozzle. The further back you cut, the larger the caulk bead will be, so decide what's appropriate for the task at hand, and cut off the tip of the nozzle at a 45° angle. Break the seal on the tube by sticking a small screwdriver into the opening of the nozzle. Finally, you're ready to apply the caulk. Squeeze the trigger and move the tip of the nozzle along the seam. You can either push or pull the gun, but pushing it forces the caulk into narrow seams more effectively. Move the gun slowly and evenly, and stop at the end of the seam. Push the nozzle into the corner, twist it, and lift it away. If you want to smooth the caulk, use a plastic spoon or a drinking straw dipped in water.

Caulk works best on cracks that are less than half an inch wide. Wider cracks generally are best filled with expandable foam or filled with some type of backing material before you caulk.

Close the gap.

You'll often find a gap between the house sill (the top of the foundation) and the siding. If that space is open, fill it with something called caulking backer rope found in the weather-stripping aisle of home centers and hardware stores. This is an incredibly simple process—you just unroll the backer rope and stuff it into the gap between the siding and the foundation. If you push the backer rope far enough into the gap, it will stay all on its own, sealing out drafts and itty-bitty critters.

Cover basement window wells.

Inexpensive, easy-to-install plastic window well covers reduce heat loss from basement windows. All you have to do is measure the widest point on the window, make a note as to whether the frame is a rectangle or a semi-circle, and then buy the appropriate cover. Most designs have an upper flange that you slip under the siding and a lower flange that you simply weigh down with medium-sized rocks. After you fasten the cover to the foundation with masonry anchors, your job is done.

Clean your lawnmower deck after each use.

The deck, or underside, of a lawnmower can become coated with grass clippings. When this happens, the blade can't turn easily, the motor has to strain, and the mower uses up more gasoline. Rinse off the deck of the mower after every usage. If necessary, use a putty knife to gently scrape away crusty bits.

Maintain your lawnmower.

Keeping the blades sharp and the oil and air filters clean helps a mower burn less gasoline and minimizes pollution. Remove the blades and take them to be sharpened once a month. Tune up your lawnmower every year before mowing season.

Use a rotary mower.

Gas-powered mowers are expensive to buy, run, and maintain. If you have a small- to medium-sized lawn, you can avoid that whole category of expenses by using a rotary mower. A rotary mower is nothing more than several blades on a spindle attached to a handle. As you push the mower, the blades spin and cut the grass. As long as you keep the blades sharp, these mowers work wonderfully. Consider this: With a rotary mower, you'd be doing something good for the planet, good for your wallet, and you wouldn't have to pay extra for the workout!

Provide shade for an air conditioning condenser.

Shading an air conditioning condenser increases its efficiency by up to 10 percent. Use shrubs, other foundation plantings or a trellis to provide adequate shade. No matter what you use, make sure you leave plenty of air space to avoid restricting airflow to the condenser.

Prune shrubs surrounding the air conditioning condenser.

Shade is a good thing, but restricted airflow is not. Prune any shrubs around your air conditioning condenser a few times every year to make sure leaves and branches don't restrict airflow to the unit.

Install a pool cover.

Putting a cover over a pool between uses reduces the evaporation of water by 90 percent and reduces the cost of heating the pool since the cover helps the pool retain heat.

Cover your spa and add a heating timer.

By covering your spa, you can keep the water warmer between uses. That way, less energy is needed to get it hot and steamy. You might also want to add a timer to your spa to automatically raise the temperature right before you typically use it. This way, you can enjoy added convenience and savings.

Chapter 10

Automobiles

With gasoline prices at or near all-time highs, everyone wants to get better gas mileage. Here are some simple, low-cost ways to start saving at the pump.

Buy a hybrid car.

Hybrid cars get as much as 50 miles to a gallon. Start by checking out www.hybridcars.com to learn more about buying, using, and maintaining a hybrid car.

Buy a more fuel-efficient car.

Consider buying a car that gets more miles to the gallon than your current vehicle. As you shop, remember that a car with a manual transmission is more fuel-efficient than one with an automatic transmission, assuming you drive it properly. A manual car with overdrive, a tachometer, or a shift indicator can save you up to 10 percent on gas! Before making a decision, go to www.epa.gov/greenvehicles, a site designed to help you choose the most fuel-efficient car to meet your needs.

Pump up your tires.

Cars use about 6 percent more gas when the tires are under-inflated, so keep those tires filled with air. If you're not sure what your tire pressure should be, look for a label somewhere on your car that provides this information. Check along the edge of the driver side door or doorjamb, inside the glove box or inside the gas cap cover. If the label shows a range, use the higher number.

QUICK TIP

When the temperature drops, check your tires. On average, tires lose about one pound per square inch (psi) for every 10°F drop in temperature.

Get a regular oil change.

Clean oil reduces the friction between moving parts, which can reduce fuel consumption by 3 percent or more.

QUICK TIP

Use the manufacturer's recommended grade of motor oil in your car and check the label before you buy a bottle to see if it bears the "Energy Conserving" symbol. This means that the American Petroleum Institute certifies that the oil contains friction-reducing additives that can improve fuel economy.

Drive slower.

For maximum fuel efficiency, drive 55 miles per hour and avoid going over 60 miles per hour whenever possible. For every 5 miles per hour added to this maximum speed, you pay an extra 10 cents a gallon in gasoline.

QUICK TIP

The easiest way to keep your speed steady is to set the cruise control whenever conditions allow.

Drive like a turtle, not a rabbit.

The standard advice for conserving gas is to avoid jackrabbit stops and starts. But what does that mean, and how do you accomplish it? Simple. Don't screech up to or away from traffic lights and stop signs. In heavy traffic, leave plenty of room between you and the car ahead of you so you can slow down gradually rather than stomping on the brakes at the last minute. When the traffic starts moving again, gradually increase your speed rather than jumping off the line like a NASCAR driver.

Replace your car's air filter.

A clogged air filter increases fuel consumption by about 10 percent, and yet it's so easy to avoid. Have your air filter checked each time you have your oil changed, and replace it as soon as it gets dirty.

Tune up your engine.

Scrupulously follow the manufacturer's recommendations regarding tune-ups. Your car can use as much as 20 percent more gasoline if it has the wrong fuel ratio, bad spark plugs, or incorrect spark timing. If that sounds like mumbo-jumbo to you, don't worry. You don't have to know what those terms mean, you only need to know a mechanic who does. Find one you trust and follow his or her suggestions.

Clear off the roof.

A loaded roof rack decreases gas mileage by as much as 5 percent. If you simply don't need that extra luggage or those mountain bikes where you're headed, save some money by removing them.

Clean out unnecessary items.

I need to practice what I preach with this tip—a person could live for a week off the stuff I have stashed in my car! Unfortunately, all that mess adds up. For every extra 100 pounds of cargo a car carries, its gas mileage is reduced by about 2 percent.

Take it easy on hills.

Don't speed up while climbing hills—the engine is already working hard to overcome gravity. If you can, use the momentum from going down one hill to help you up the next.

Close the windows.

This may surprise you, but in most circumstances, it costs less to run the air conditioner than it does to open the windows! Open car windows increase drag and reduce your mileage by 10 percent.

Use your vents instead of the air conditioner.

If you need some fresh air, keep the windows closed and use the vent. This should keep you comfortable enough while driving in moderate weather and saves you the expense of running the air conditioner.

Cover a truck bed.

Pick-ups may be extremely handy, but they're not very aerodynamic. Air flows over the cab and down into the bed, where it pushes against the tailgate and creates drag. A bed cover improves the aerodynamics of a truck and pays for itself with better gas mileage.

Wash and wax your car.

A clean, slick surface slides through the air with less drag. That means less work for your car.

Buy the right gasoline.

Use the type of gas recommended by the car's manufacturer, usually a type with detergent additives. Don't buy more expensive gas than the automaker recommends—it won't improve your gas mileage, it will only increase the cost of operating your vehicle.

Don't idle for long.

When you're waiting in the car for any length of time—for your kids to get out of school, a friend to come out to the car, your mate to run into the convenience store—turn off the ignition. You'll save a substantial amount of gas over time.

Resist the drive-thru.

Avoid drive-thru windows with long lines. It only takes a few extra minutes to park and go inside a bank, restaurant, or drug store, but it can save you lots of money over time.

Use a timer with your engine-block heater.

Engine-block heaters are a great way to make sure your car starts in extremely cold weather, but they can be unnecessarily expensive. Put a timer on the heater and set it to operate during the coldest part of the night and only as long as necessary.

Be skeptical of outrageous claims or expensive gas-saving devices.

The EPA has recently tested over one hundred "gas-saving" devices and found that very few improve gas mileage at all. For a full list of tested products, visit www.epa.gov/otaq/consumer/reports.htm.

HELPFUL RESOURCES

The Alliance to Save Energy
1200 18th Street NW
Suite 900
Washington, DC 20036
(202) 857-0666
www.ase.org

Database of State Incentives for Renewable Energy
www.dsireusa.org

Energy Efficiency and Renewable Energy Clearinghouse (EREC)
1-800-DOE-EREC (1-800-363-3732)
www.eren.doe.gov

ENERGY STAR Programs Hotline
& Distribution (MS-6202J)
1200 Pennsylvania Ave NW
Washington, DC 20460
(888) STAR-YES
www.energystar.gov

ENERGYguide
16 Laurel Ave. Suite 100
Wellesley Hills, MA 02481
(781) 694-3300
www.energyguide.com

Home Energy Saver
www.hes.lbl.gov

Home heating and air conditioning information
www.warmair.com

Hybrid car information
www.hybridcars.com

Partnership for Home Energy Efficiency
www.energysavers.gov

Stop Global Warming
Presidio Building 1014
San Francisco, CA 94129
www.stopglobalwarming.org

The U.S. Department of Energy
Consumer's Guide to Energy Efficiency and Renewable Energy
www.eere.energy.gov/consumer

The U.S. Environmental Protection Agency
Ariel Rios Building
1200 Pennsylvania Avenue, N.W.
Washington, DC 20460
(202) 272-0167
www.epa.gov

Gas Saving and Emission Reduction Devices Evaluation
www.epa.gov/otaq/consumer/reports.htm

Green Vehicle Guide
www.epa.gov/greenvehicles

About the Author

Jerri Farris is the author of Home Improvement 101, IdeaWise Bathrooms, IdeaWise Kitchens, IdeaWise Porches, 10-Minute Home Repairs, and dozens of other books on home improvement and home décor. Her son is in the Navy, her daughter is in college, and she now lives in Independence. (Missouri, that is.)